ALL-PRO FOOTBALL STARS '81

JERRY BRONDFIELD

D0331319

SCHOLASTIC BOOK SERVICES
New York Toronto London Auckland Sydney Tokyo

Cover photo: Brian Sipe of Cleveland Browns

ISBN 0-590-32206-0

12 11 10 9 8 7 6 5 4 3 2 1   9   1 2 3 4 5 6/8

Printed in the U. S. A.   01

CONTENTS

The Bears' Walter Payton bursts through the defense.

ALL-PRO
OFFENSE
1980

TE: **Kellen Winslow**, San Diego Chargers
WR: **John Jefferson**, San Diego Chargers
WR: **Charlie Joiner**, San Diego Chargers
 T: **Leon Gray**, Houston Oilers
 T: **Mike Kenn**, Atlanta Falcons
 G: **Joe DeLamielleure**, Cleveland Browns
 G: **John Hannah**, New England Patriots
 C: **Mike Webster**, Pittsburgh Steelers
 Q: **Brian Sipe**, Cleveland Browns
RB: **Earl Campbell**, Houston Oilers
RB: **Walter Payton**, Chicago Bears

Tight End
KELLEN WINSLOW
6-5½, 252
SAN DIEGO CHARGERS

Never has the same NFL team had the two best wide receivers and the best tight end in the league. But the Chargers had 'em in John Jefferson, Charlie Joiner, and Kellen Winslow. But Winslow almost wasn't a Charger. One minute before the deadline for the first round in the 1979 draft, the Chargers made a deal with the Cleveland Browns to get him. For the Chargers it was a moment of destiny.

As a rookie, everything pointed toward a great career for Winslow, who had been a star at Missouri, where he caught 71 passes for 1,089 yards and 10 TDs. Winslow, a tremendous physical specimen with great speed, started for the Chargers as a rookie and was leading the club in receptions when he broke a leg in the seventh game and was lost for the rest of the year.

The big question: Would the leg heal for 1980 and allow him to take up where he'd left off? Did it ever! Winslow was *better* than ever as Dan Fouts, The Chargers' great QB, found the big target in or out of a crowd. If the ball was anywhere near him, Winslow would get it — plus a few more yards when he'd drag or bowl over the unlucky cornerback who hit him. For the year Winslow had 89 receptions, 1,290 yards, and 13 TDs. Not only was he such a dangerous threat via the air, but as a blocker on the running plays he was one of the best straight-ahead blasters among NFL tight ends. Look for many All-Pro repeat performances out of this guy.

Wide Receiver

JOHN JEFFERSON

6-1, 184

SAN DIEGO CHARGERS

There are three ways to describe the way John Jefferson catches the ball: merely great; downright dazzling; or, in many cases, miraculously. When Jefferson puts together his great speed, his brilliant pass routes, his glue-fingered hands, and his ability to get loose from a defender, he's just the best in the business. Maybe the best, ever.

When QB Dan Fouts needs a big hunk of yardage fast, all he has to say to Jefferson in the huddle is: "Okay, Jeff, get loose, hang loose, give 'em a head shake, and I'll present you with the ball."

A lot of people throughout the league knew it was going to happen from Jefferson's rookie year on. He was a unanimous All-Rookie choice in 1978 and All-Pro stardom was a cinch for the future.

His stats for last season are eye-popping. As the number one receiver in the NFL he hauled in 82 catches for 1,340 yards and 13 TDs.

As a rookie he'd been the first NFL newcomer to gain at least 1,000 yards receiving in almost 10 years (since the Eagles' Harold Jackson in 1969). The Chargers drafted him after he'd caught 175 passes for 2,824 yards at Arizona State. They checked the films, saw his blazing speed and the nifty way he ran pass routes, and all the coaches whistled at once. There was no doubt in anyone's mind that Jefferson would make the starting team from game one. Not many receivers make All-Pro in third season. There's too much talent around at that spot. With Jefferson, it was no surprise.

Wide Receiver
CHARLIE JOINER
5-11, 183
SAN DIEGO CHARGERS

Nobody ever waited as long as Charlie Joiner did to make All-Pro. It took him 12 years. But nobody is saying he doesn't deserve it, now that he has the honor. Joiner was only a fourth-round draft pick by Houston in 1969, and the Oilers saw him as a defensive back. He'd been a fine receiver at Grambling University in Louisiana, but the Oilers were desperate for defensive backs.

But Joiner had such great hands and ran such brilliant pass patterns that the Oilers quickly put him back into a receiver's spot. After three seasons he was a victim of a trade that sent him to Cincinnati, where he was a fine receiver for three more years. But he wasn't grabbing big headlines, and nobody ever saw him as a potential All-Pro. Another trade and Charlie Joiner became a Charger.

Now he had one of the NFL's finest QBs in Dan Fouts throwing to him. For the next four years he was one of the most dangerous receivers in the NFL. In 1979 he was nothing short of sensational, catching 72 passes for 1,008 yards. This past season, with Fouts having his pick of three great receivers to throw to, Joiner again cracked the 1,000-yard plateau with 71 receptions and 1,132 yards. Together Joiner, Jefferson, and Winslow caught 242 passes for 3,762 yards, an all-time record for receivers on the same team.

Offensive Tackle
LEON GRAY
6-3, 260
HOUSTON OILERS

By now it's habit-forming with Leon Gray. It's the third straight All-Pro year for the squared-off hunk of granite who masquerades as an offensive tackle. Gray is also that rare lineman who has been picked All-Pro for two different clubs. His first selection was in 1978 with New England. Traded to the Oilers in 1979, he picked up right where he'd left off. No one was more pleased than the Oilers' coaching staff, who watched him block ferociously and put out such great pass-protection for Oilers' QBs.

But football almost lost Gray to music. When Leon Gray played the trumpet in his Mississippi high school band, he was excused from 10 band appearances each year. Those were the Friday nights he played tackle for the football team. Gray took his football skills to Jackson State College, Mississippi, but left his trumpet home.

Gray started for four years at Jackson State and became a third-round draft choice by the Miami Dolphins. The Dolphins soon made a mistake. They cut him in camp and put him on waivers. The New England Patriots grabbed him right after the final cut.

Gray started the last eight games of the year for the Patriots as a rookie. He was definitely one of the NFL's future stars.

Soon Gray became known for his pass-blocking abilities. He was already a powerful blocker on running plays. Throughout the NFL, the defenses knew it wasn't going to be easy getting through to sack the QB.

Often Gray's the difference between a completion, an incompletion, or an interception. Or in getting the QB's head knocked off.

9

Offensive Tackle
MIKE KENN
6-6, 257
ATLANTA FALCONS

It was really only a matter of time before the starry label: All-Pro would be pinned on Mike Kenn. At Michigan, where he was All-Big Ten, the pro scouts kept saying: "Now, if he can only add 15 or 20 pounds to that frame he could be a terror." So, Kenn added 15 pounds to his frame by the time he reported to the Falcons training camp. The Falcons, who were wise enough to make him a first-round draft choice, were delighted.

Kenn was intelligent and very coachable. His coaches liked his quick feet, which are so important in getting back for pass protection, and he had great balance on his drive-blocking technique. Kenn started every game as a rookie and was a unanimous choice for the 1979 All-Rookie team.

By his third year as a pro, everyone around the league was convinced that Kenn was going to be a problem for the defense for the next few seasons. "There's no question about it," says Leeman Bennett, the Falcons' head coach. "Mike Kenn is already one of the dominant tackles in the NFL — and he's going to get better."

Bill Andrews, Atlanta's great ball carrier, knows that Kenn will nearly always get him some sort of opening on a running play over Mike's position. "The confidence I have in Mike," says Andrews, "is worth an extra yard on every pop."

In his leisure time around home, Kenn enjoys quite a reputation as a fine cook. Invitations to dinner at his place are greatly prized. Mike Kenn also has the recipe for continued greatness in the NFL.

Offensive Guard

JOE DeLAMIELLEURE

6-3, 250
Cleveland Browns

Joe DeLamielleure now is the first offensive guard to make All-Pro six straight years. And like Leon Gray of Houston, he is the rare case of a player making All-Pro with two different clubs. Traded by Buffalo to the Browns last year, Joe was a big factor in Cleveland's surge to the playoffs.

Joe DeLamielleure always gets his man! When he was at Michigan State he majored in criminal justice. "I wish he'd have gone into crime busting instead of football," said an NFL linebacker. "When he comes out to lead interference you can just see that steely glint in his eye as he concentrates on getting his man."

A first-round draft choice in 1973, DeLamielleure became an immediate starter for the Buffalo Bills and made the All-Rookie team. It took him only two years to make the jump to All-Pro. But the way he leads interference and drops back for pass protection, everyone agreed he'd make it soon. He's also a ferocious straight-ahead blocker on running plays. "I love to run behind Joe," O.J. Simpson said when he was with the Bills. "He's the kind of blocker a ballcarrier should remember in his will."

DeLamielleure made the All-Big Ten team in college three times, and topped it off with All-America in his senior year. With his sixth straight year as an All-Pro in the record book, why not try for seven?

Joe has one more distinction going for him. He has one of the toughest names to spell in the NFL.

Offensive Guard
JOHN HANNAH
6-2, 265
New England Patriots

John Hannah has great respect for Joe DeLamielleure and wishes him well. But Hannah has been named All-Pro five straight years and is determined to keep his string going — especially if Joe falters one of these years and fails to make the honor team. In putting together his own string, Hannah brings strength, mental and physical toughness, desire, and intelligence to the job. Hannah has 'em all.

A lot of the Patriots' ground-gaining came over Hannah's position, where he was a tremendous straight-ahead blocker. But Hannah carried out his other chores equally well. He was super at pulling out to block on wide plays, and he gave QB Steve Grogan excellent protection on passes.

Some people thought Hannah would have trouble in the pros after starring at Alabama. Because Alabama used a wishbone offense, Hannah did all his blocking straight ahead. What would happen when he had to do so many different things in the pros? But 'Bama coach Bear Bryant said Hannah was the best lineman he'd ever had. "Don't worry about ol' Ham Hocks [Hannah's nickname]," said Bryant. "He'll do it all."

Bryant was right, of course. Hannah became a starter as a rookie and made the All-Rookie team after being drafted on the first round in 1973. Except for one game in his first season, he's started every game for the Patriots since then. Look for that new All-Pro record for ol' Ham Hocks.

Center
MIKE WEBSTER
6-1½, 250
Pittsburgh Steelers

Dependable. Say it again: DEPENDA-
BLE. Always making the perfect snap.
Always carrying out his assignment,
whether it's blocking or pass-protecting.
It's the third straight year as All-Pro for
the Steelers' super center and nobody
questioned the choice.

The Steelers didn't select Webster until
the sixth round of the draft a few years
ago — which isn't very high. But the
Steelers' coaches had him figured for two
positions: guard or center. That way he
had two chances. Actually he made good
at both. He was an All-Rookie choice at
center, but a year later, in 1976, he split
the season at both posts. The following
season he became the Steelers' center —
for good. And better than good is the way
to describe the former Wisconsin star.

He handles all snaps, not just to the
quarterback but also the longer ones for
punts and place-kicks. Many centers can't
do that. And when getting it into QB Terry
Bradshaw's hands, he's a master of split-
second timing. It's the best exchange in
the NFL.

After the snap, Webster blocks with
great ferocity and quickness. Even when
the defense plays a man right over him,
he isn't afraid of the slap to the head that
all centers must expect. He also has two
other talents. He has the quick feet needed
when a center drops back to give his QB
pass protection. And on punts, after snap-
ing the ball, he's one of the first downfield
to close in on the punt returner. What it
adds up to is All-Pro performance without
weakness.

Quarterback
BRIAN SIPE
6-1, 195
Cleveland Browns

Okay, we hear you screaming about Terry Bradshaw, Dan Fouts, and one or two others, but there's no getting around the fact that last year the best all-around QB in the NFL was the Browns' Brian Sipe. For the last two years Sipe has been overshadowed by more glamorous names, but nearly every coach in the NFL and the vast majority of sports writers who cover the league agreed that Sipe was the QB of the year since he almost took the Browns to the Super Bowl. Only an upset loss to Oakland in zero-degree weather in the AFC playoffs kept them from a crack at the biggie.

The Browns were considered a middle-of-the-pack club as the year opened but behind the brilliant passing and leadership of Sipe, they were the surprise of the season. All Sipe did was pass for 340 receptions, 4,132 yards, and 30 TDs.

More importantly he provided the leadership that carried the Browns to several last-quarter victories. Occupying that spot was a surprise in itself. Sipe was only a 13th-round draft choice in 1972, out of San Diego State. He spent two years on the "taxi squad," being ready if needed, but not even dressing for games. Then came two more years understudying Mike Phipps. Finally, in the 1976 opener, Phipps was injured and Sipe stepped in. He's never stepped out, except for injuries in 1977 for a few weeks.

Sipe has had a half dozen 300-yard games, passing, and is considered one of the best rushers among QBs in the NFL. He reads defenses quickly, spots his receivers in a flash, and delivers the ball right on the numbers. He's a welcome newcomer to stardom.

EARL CAMPBELL
5-11, 225
Houston Oilers

    Here's the problem: how do you say anything about Earl Campbell that hasn't been said before? For the third straight year he led the NFL in rushing, and for the third straight year he improved his own statistics. His 1,934 yards rushing in 1980 is second only to O.J. Simpson's all-time season mark of 2,003. Do you want to bet he will break The Juice's record someday?

Listen to Dwight White, Steeler linebacker: "Earl Campbell is almost illegal. When he hits that hole it's like a door slamming. Earl Campbell is a Larry Csonka and O.J. Simpson combined." Some of the things other players say about the Oilers' rookie aren't printable.

Any way you look at it, Earl Campbell is the most exciting runner in the NFL in years. A unanimous All-America at the University of Texas, the Heisman winner was the Oilers' first draft pick two years ago after rushing for 4,444 yards as a Longhorn. Oh, he was super, all right, but would he bring all that talent to the pros? He brought it — and it was the reason the Oilers made the playoffs for the first time in their history in 1978.

Moving like a runaway freight train, Campbell uses his brute power and great speed to run around tacklers or run over them if he has to. Often he is hit by three or four people, but breaks the tackles and continues on for four, five, or ten yards more. Defensive backs find his speed deceptive. He would be into the secondary before they are set to hit him. And often it is too late.

Campbell is squarely on a course to break the legendary Jim Brown's lifetime mark of 12,312 yards.

WALTER PAYTON

5-11, 211
Chicago Bears

At the end of the 1979 season Walter Payton was very upset. He'd been an All-Pro running back in 1976-77-78, but in 1979 he'd lost the honor to Ottis Anderson of the St. Louis Cardinals.

So, last season, Walter Payton cranked

up for a bit of extra effort every time he blasted into the line. He seemed to find a new burst of speed any time he broke into the clear. Walter Payton was determined to regain his all-star status. NFL tacklers are still nursing the bruises that Payton left on them.

There's no doubt that the Jackson State, (Miss.) graduate, who was a first-round draft pick for the Bears in 1975, will go down in history as one of the game's greatest runners.

Last year Payton captured his fifth straight NFL rushing title with 1,460 yards on 317 carries. His 8,386 yards in his first six seasons already place him fifth on the NFL career list. His 42 100-yard games tie O.J. Simpson, and puts him second to the legendary Jim Brown's record of 58.

"It isn't just his speed," says one NFL coach. "It's his blinding quickness. A lot of guys can stop on a dime, but how many can be off, full speed, on their first step?"

And a veteran NFL defensive back says: "He seems to come at you from all directions. I swear, he doesn't know himself which way he's going to cut."

His favorite maneuver looks like a broken play. He'll sweep right, see that he's cut off, and will stop and bolt all the way back to the left side. There won't be a blocker with him, but somehow he'll slice free for big yardage.

"The name of the game is confidence," says Payton. "I told them when I came up that I'd make it. Some people didn't listen because I wasn't all that big."

Big doesn't always mean better.

Denver Bronco linebacker, Randy Gradishar, fills the hole and focuses on ball-carrier coming at him.

ALL-PRO DEFENSE 1980

E: **Lee Roy Selmon,** Tampa Bay Buccaneers
E: **Art Still,** Kansas City Chiefs
T: **Randy White,** Dallas Cowboys
T: **Gary Johnson,** San Diego Chargers
LB: **Ted Hendricks,** Oakland Raiders
LB: **Randy Gradishar,** Denver Broncos
LB: **Robert Brazile,** Houston Oilers
CB: **Lemar Parrish,** Washington Redskins
CB: **Lester Hayes,** Oakland Raiders
S: **Donnie Shell,** Pittsburgh Steelers
S: **Nolan Cromwell,** Los Angeles Rams

Defensive End
LEE ROY SELMON
6-3, 255
Tampa Bay Buccaneers

Before his career is over, Lee Roy Selmon may be recognized as the finest all-around defensive end ever to hit the NFL. And "hit" is the right word. It's what Lee Roy is famous for, whether it's racking up the ballcarrier or sacking the QB. It all adds up to his second straight honor year.

It was a big jump from college stardom to success as a pro, and it's a risky business pinning "can't miss" labels on a rookie. There was no risk when they pinned it on Selmon. One of three All-America brothers at Oklahoma, Selmon was a first-round draft choice for the new team Bucs five years ago. His strength and agility made him an instant starter and won him All-Rookie acclaim.

Two years later there was no way anyone could keep him off the All-Pro team. "He's the best defensive end against the run I've ever seen," says Buc coach John McKay. True, true! Nobody puts a full block on him when he's angling in on the ballcarrier. And once he gets his hands on the guy, the guy has gone as far as he's going on that play.

Selmon is a fierce pass rusher. As often as not he goes right over the blocker, instead of circling around him, on his way to the quarterback. Once, against Buffalo, he actually threw two blockers into the Bills' QB, Joe Ferguson, to make the sack. "Most amazing defensive play I ever saw," said Buffalo sports writer, Larry Felser.

Give Selmon a little more time and he'll make even more amazing plays. After all, he hasn't even reached his prime.

Defensive End
ART STILL
6-5, 252
Kansas City Chiefs

When NFL scouts took a look at the 1978 draft prospects, they all agreed on a "can't miss" label for a huge Kentucky defensive end named Art Still. Still had been an All-America at Kentucky. His college major was in Criminology, and he considered it a crime for a ballcarrier to make any yardage around his end. Art Still punished all the ball-carrying criminals who tried him.

So sure of his potential were the NFL scouts that the Chiefs knew they'd have to take him early in the draft. So early, in fact, that Still was the second player named in the entire draft — ahead of a lot of glittering quarterbacks and running backs.

From Day One in the Chiefs' camp they knew they'd have to regard him as a starter, even as a rookie. Nobody was surprised when he was named to the All-Rookie team in 1978.

As a three-year veteran last season, Still's skills were the talk of the league. He had great agility to go with his mountainous size. He could hand-fight the blockers and still get to the runner. For three years he has led the Chiefs in quarterback sacks. Frequently the enemy will put two blockers on him, which leaves another Chief free to make the stop. There wasn't an apparent weakness in his all-around, super-defensive play. And there's no reason why he won't make All-Pro a habit-forming thing.

Defensive Tackle
RANDY WHITE
6-4, 252
Dallas Cowboys

What've we got here? A perennial All-Pro? It looks like it with Randy White, who now has nailed down the honor for the third straight season. White is just entering his prime and barring injuries he's on the verge of super stardom.

White has been around, defensively, but now he has finally found a home. He was an All-America defensive end at Maryland, but when the Cowboys made him a first-round draft choice five years ago, they made him a linebacker. Why not? He was big, strong, and very agile. In fact, he was downright quick. And mean. And determined. And intense. And he liked to hit ballcarriers. See what we mean?

But although he started some games his first two years, he also served as a backup. Coach Tom Landry decided on a switch. Because of his quickness and great strength, White would also make a great pass rusher at tackle, where he could be used all the time.

So, Randy White, in 1977, went into his third defensive position. He took to the job immediately and had a great season.

But 1978 saw him developing into stardom. Quarterbacks around the league were fleeing for their lives as White put the pressure on them. When he wasn't sacking them he was making them get rid of the ball before they really wanted to. Meanwhile, he was making his share of tackles. Blockers rarely made him take a backward step.

What Randy White had become was the perfect defensive tackle.

Defensive Tackle
GARY JOHNSON
6-3, 252
San Diego Chargers

When Gary Johnson was in the eighth grade back in Bossier City, La., his pals nicknamed him "Big Hands." Those hands kept gorwing — along with the rest of him. At Grambling University those hands helped make him an All-America and got the pro scouts talking about his strength and quickness. . . . The Chargers lost no time in claiming him in 1975 (first round). About ninety percent of the defensive tackles in the NFL were bigger than Johnson, but there weren't many rookies with his potential.

Very quickly in pre-season camp, Johnson showed he was a terror for an offensive lineman to take on. The pre-season exhibition games brought gleams to the eyes of the Chargers' defensive line coaches. In the second quarter of the second regular season game in 1975, the rookie replaced an injured starter and nobody ever got him out of the lineup after that.

By 1979 Johnson was selected for the AFC Pro Bowl squad, but he vowed that wasn't honor enough for him. Last year the Chargers' defense pivoted around him as they fought their way to the playoffs and everyone agreed that Gary Johnson was among the two or three defensive tackles in the NFL and deserved to be All-Pro.

Linebacker
TED HENDRICKS
6-7, 225
Oakland Raiders

There's no end to the interesting things you can say about Ted Hendricks. That he was born in Guatemala City, Guatemala.

That he is the tallest linebacker in NFL history. That he holds the NFL record (20) for blocked punts, field goals, and points-after-touchdown. That he's called "The Mad Stork," a nickname he hates.

He was drafted out of Miami (Fla.) University by Baltimore in 1969, on the second round.

As a defensive end he was a two-time All-America in 1967-68. His long legs, flapping arms, and frenzied play made him a distinctive sight. He was also distinctive enough to win the Knute Rockne Trophy as the nation's outstanding lineman.

With the Colts in 1969, he became a starter in the sixth game of the season and has played in 178 straight games with three different clubs. The Colts had needed help at linebacker and gambled that Hendricks could make the switch from end. Athletes at 6-7 often aren't very agile. They can't switch direction in a flash, the way a linebacker must. Hendricks was the exception. Within two years he was a unanimous All-Pro linebacker. Then the Colts made a mistake, and traded him to the Green Bay Packers.

With the Packers he was All-Pro every year for four years. He has blocked field goals, punts, and PATs. He intercepts passes. He has picked up a fumble and raced for a TD. He sacks quarterbacks and turns back sweeps. Anything an outside linebacker is supposed to do, Ted Hendricks does. In 1975, he joined the Raiders as a free agent. And last year he was a big factor in the Raiders' miracle march to the Super Bowl.

Linebacker
RANDY GRADISHAR
6-3, 223
Denver Broncos

It's the third straight All-Pro honor for the Broncos' Mister Busy. And there are few critics who'd say he hasn't earned it.

Gradishar plays the middle linebacker spot for the Broncos, which means he has to cover a lot of ground. Anything that comes over the middle or to either side of him is his responsibility. If the outside linebackers get fooled or taken out of the play, the middle man has to cover. With his great speed and zest for the ball, Gradishar seems to be flying all over the place.

He attracted all the pro scouts' attention as an All-America at Ohio State. Woody Hayes, the Buckeyes' former coach, tagged him as ". . . the best linebacker I've ever seen." He'd been a three-year starter for the Bucks and an All-America, but the Bronco coaches held their breath a bit. He'd had a complicated knee operation after his final college season and only time would tell if it were successful. Other clubs decided to pass him up. The Broncos gambled and grabbed him on the first round of the 1974 draft.

The knee held up. Gradishar got in a lot of playing time his rookie year and became a starter — and a star — in his second season. He has been the Broncos' leader in tackles the last four seasons. And with his speed and savvy he's a dangerous defender against the pass. As the TV announcers like to say: "He does it all."

Linebacker
ROBERT BRAZILE
6-4, 230
Houston Oilers

Sometime in a pro player's career, he's bound to have a bad game. Chalk it up to bad luck, injuries, the weather, or a meal that didn't set well. But in six years in the NFL nobody has ever seen Bob Brazile play a bad game. And it'll be a long time coming.

In 1975, Brazile was not only a unanimous NFL All-Rookie but also was named Defensive Rookie of the Year. All the experts said that if they had to pick one newcomer who was a cinch to become a future All-Pro, they'd have to pick Brazile. With that kind of start, Brazile decided not to let anybody down. Especially himself.

An All-America at Jackson State, Mississippi, Brazile was a first-round draft pick by the Oilers. There were a few critics who said Brazile was too tall, at 6-4, for a linebacker. Guys that tall weren't able to react and change direction as nimbly as shorter players. The ideal linebacker, they said, was 6-2. Brazile soon made a lot of people think 6-4 was ideal.

Not only was he a deadly tackler, but he had the upper body strength that linebackers need to ward off blockers. And, as for quick reactions, Brazile's 4.6 speed for 40 yards is the fastest for any linebacker in the NFL. Seldom is he faked out on a play. Rarely is he blocked out. Never does he fail to stop a runner once he gets his hands on him. He's been chosen All-Pro five times since he broke in. Nobody is saying there'll never be a sixth time.

Cornerback
LEMAR PARRISH
5-10, 183
WASHINGTON REDSKINS

Lemar Parrish is one of the smallest defensive backs in the NFL, but he does one of the biggest jobs. "The guy is all heart and desire," says one long-time NFL coach. "He doesn't know the meaning of the word 'fear,' and I've seen him take on the biggest running backs and tight ends, one-on-one and make the play."

Parrish is also proof of the value of good, old-fashioned American "plugging away." Parrish believed in himself and kept working at being the best cornerback in the NFL. It took him 10 years to convince the experts he was All-Pro material and in 1979 he made it after being selected for the Pro Bowl six times. Last year everyone agreed he was a repeater.

Parrish, from little Lincoln College in Missouri, broke into the NFL as merely a seventh-round draft choice with the Cincinnati Bengals in 1970. By the following season he was a regular, and a rising star. Bengal fans were shocked when he was traded to Washington in 1978, but Redskin fans were delighted from his very first game with the "Skins." A teeth-rattling tackler with a nose for the ball, he protected his zone against enemy passes with all-out fury.

He also broke his hand in the eighth game of that first season with Washington, but after three weeks of rest he insisted that he be put back in the lineup wearing a cast on his hand. He played the last three games of the season that way.

Cornerback
LESTER HAYES
6-0, 195
OAKLAND RAIDERS

One of the qualities NFL coaches look for in cornerbacks is toughness — mental and physical. When the Raiders took Lester Hayes as a fifth-round draft pick in 1977, they knew he'd been a small, 192-pound linebacker for two years at Texas A&M, before being switched to the defensive backfield. You've got to be tough to survive as a linebacker in the Southwest Conference when you're that small.

Hayes also had great speed so the Raiders figured his future lay in the defensive secondary where he could match swift receivers stride for stride. Late in his rookie season, Hayes became a starter. Since then, the word was out that NFL receivers would have a tough time earning their pay in Hayes's territory.

Hayes has the rare ability to sense which way a receiver is going to cut. He never gets caught flat-footed, and nobody beats him deep. Once the ball is in the air the ex-linebacker feels challenged: "If I can't pick it off I'll settle for batting it down. If I just bat it down, though, I feel disappointed."

It's that kind of attitude that makes a cornerback a candidate for All-Pro. Last year the critics decided that Lester Hayes was one of the two best in the NFL at his job.

Safety
DONNIE SHELL
5-11, 190
PITTSBURGH STEELERS

The Steelers didn't make it to the Super Bowl last year as most fans expected them to. But don't blame it on Donnie Shell. Shell performed as usual — which means that he gave 110% of his brilliant, all-around talent.

It was the second straight year on the All-Pro team for Shell, but he had to convince a lot of people before he ever got a chance to be a Steeler.

Although Shell had a sparkling college career at South Carolina State, the pros weren't even interested enough in 1974 to draft him. But Shell knocked on the Steeler's door and said, "Hey, look me over as a free agent." It cost the Steelers nothing but a plane ticket to take a look. They liked what they saw in camp and signed him.

The Steelers had been having problems covering enemy tight ends who were fast and big. Shell had the speed and the courage to meet them head-on. He was in and out of the line-up mostly as a Special Teams player for three years and finally the Steelers had to admit he was not only good enough to stick around but to start. In 1977 he became a regular. Frankly, most of the teams in the NFL wondered why it took the Steelers so long to realize they had a budding star.

In 1979 the budding star burst into full brilliance. Tough, quick, and smart, Shell has been the glue that holds the Steelers' defensive secondary together.

NOLAN CROMWELL

6-1, 198

LOS ANGELES RAMS

Let's get one thing out of the way. Nolan Cromwell is probably the best athlete in the NFL. By that we mean all-around agility, reactions, fluidity, speed, coordination, and strength. When the Rams made him a second-round draft choice in 1977, they weren't sure what they'd do with him. At the University of Kansas he'd played two years as a super safety and two years as a brilliant quarterback. He was not only a pip of a passer but was the best running QB in the nation.

Cromwell was also a super track athlete — a record-holding hurdler and a top decathlon performer. When the Rams got him they used him on specialty teams the first year. Finally, in 1979, there was no way he could be kept out of the starting lineup and he immediately showed some of the best potential in the NFL as a safety. His crunching tackling and defense against the pass got rave reviews throughout the league.

In 1980, Nolan Cromwell displayed such all-around brilliance that he was a unanimous choice for All-Pro. And he's young enough to wear all-star status for many seasons to come. Welcome to the big-time, Nolan Cromwell!

ALL-ROOKIE OFFENSE 1980

TE: **Junior Miller:** Atlanta Falcons
WR: **Art Monk,** Washington Redskins
WR: **Ray Butler,** Baltimore Colts
 T: **Anthony Munoz,** Cincinnati Bengals
 T: **Stan Brock,** New Orleans Saints
 G: **Ray Snell,** Tampa Bay Buccaneers
 G: **Tyrone McGriff,** Pittsburgh Steelers
 C: **Tom Ginn,** Detroit Lions
 Q: **David Woodley,** Miami Dolphins
RB: **Billy Sims,** Detroit Lions
RB: **Joe Cribbs,** Buffalo Bills

Tight End
JUNIOR MILLER
6-4, 235
ATLANTA FALCONS

It isn't often that a pro team makes a tight end it's first-round draft pick — but how often does a Junior Miller show up? Falcon scouts had called the Nebraska All-America "the best pure tight end prospect in a decade." By "pure tight end" they meant great physical size, good speed, sticky hands, fierce blocking ability, and the instincts of a runaway water buffalo once he catches the ball. Miller averaged 18.4 yards per reception in college (which is super) and 13 of his 61 receptions went for TDs. Meanwhile, he was knocking defensive linemen into the next county while blocking for the Cornhusker running game. Coaches in the Big Eight were sick of watching him outrun their defensive backs. Miller was an immediate starter for the Falcons after enjoying a brilliant pre-season camp. And nobody in the NFL was surprised at his success once the regular season began. His super rookie year was just a starting point for future pro greatness.

49

Wide Receiver
ART MONK
6-2, 210
WASHINGTON REDSKINS

NFL coaches always hunger for wide receivers who are not only fast but big. Heavy-duty receivers can usually get that extra yard or two after being hit by a cornerback or safety. The Redskins got the ideal package when they quickly selected Art Monk, of Syracuse, in the first round of the draft. Monk, who was a New York State and national schoolboy hurdles champ in high school, has a gliding stride which serves him well when he runs pass patterns — and he runs them brilliantly. At Syracuse he set school records for receiving with 102 catches for 1,644 yards. He was also a threat as a running back, averaging a nifty 4.5 per carry. The Redskins knew exactly what they would do with the Syracuse All-American and quickly worked him into their aerial offense in training camp. By the time the regular season began, Monk was a solid bet to make a lot of trouble for NFL defenders. His 58 receptions and 797 yards for his rookie season were just the beginning of his very bright future.

Wide Receiver
RAY BUTLER
6-3, 190
BALTIMORE COLTS

Ray Butler was almost an afterthought in the college draft. The Colts waited until the fourth round before selecting the former Southern California receiver and punt returner. Being tagged that late usually rates only a "possibility" in the coaches' minds. By the time the pre-season games were half gone, the Colts retagged Butler as a "probability." Butler had good but not blazing speed, but he quickly showed he could run brilliant pass routes. No hesitation. No mistakes in his patterns. No fear of getting nailed by fierce cornerbacks. Add a sticky pair of hands to his abilities and you've got a receiver any quarterback can count on. The Colts' Bert Jones showed no hesitancy in going to the slim rookie and Butler soon found steady employment. He fooled some of the best defensive backs in the NFL as he wound up with 34 receptions and 574 yards. And everyone thinks better days are ahead.

Offensive Tackle
ANTHONY MUNOZ
6-5, 278
CINCINNATI BENGALS

When Anthony Munoz was a senior at Southern Cal, he tore up the ligaments in his left knee in the opening game of the 1979 season. He missed the last 10 games of the regular season but came back for the Rose Bowl game against Ohio State. Bengal scouts didn't worry about that knee as they made him their first-round draft choice. They were right not to worry. The biggest lineman in Bengal history came to camp strong as an ox and, according to Bengal coach, Forrest Gregg, "He moves better and has more speed than any big man I've ever seen." When Gregg saw Munoz knock down a defensive lineman with one arm, he knew he had a starter and a potential superstar in his mammoth rookie. Munoz, who, incidentally, also pitched for the Southern Cal baseball team, was a natural athlete. He had the strength to sustain straight-ahead blocks and had great lateral and backward mobility for pass protection. Three games into the pro season, every NFL defensive line coach knew there'd be a problem handling the huge rookie.

Offensive Tackle
STAN BROCK
6-6, 275
NEW ORLEANS SAINTS

If there's no place for the Saints to go but up, Stan Brock is one of the guys who'll show them the way. The Saints knew what they were doing when they made Brock a first-round draft choice. The huge rookie from Colorado had the right blood line: his older brother, also from Colorado, plays center for the New England Patriots and was also a first-round choice. Chuck Fairbanks, the Colorado coach, merely said: "Stan Brock was the best pass blocker in college football his senior year . . . and has the best potential of any offensive lineman I've ever worked with — college or pro. . . ." The Saints, of course, had scouted the monster on their own and couldn't wait to see if everyone was right about his chances. Everyone was right. Brock, even though a rookie, blew out a few dozen of the NFL's best defensive linemen and gave QB Archie Manning some A-Plus pass protection. He has quick feet, the strength of an ox, intelligence, and great pride in doing the job right.

Offensive Guard
RAY SNELL
6-3, 255
TAMPA BAY BUCCANEERS

Way back when Ray Snell was in junior high school he played the clarinet in a band that performed at the Baltimore Colts' home games. He was considered an outstanding musician — but he'd decided, even then, that he'd rather play on the football field than in a band. Eventually he went off to the University of Wisconsin and became an All-Big Ten tackle, with super blocking ability. He sometimes lined up at tight end. Whichever side he lined up on, the Badgers always got a good gain. As a three-year starter for the Badgers, Snell attracted a lot of pro scouts. Tampa Bay decided to go high on him, and picked him off in the first round. With his quickness they tabbed him as a guard who could either block straight ahead or move out to lead the ballcarrier on a sweep. Snell's switch to guard in pre-season camp was right on target. He made the move with no difficulty and impressed every coach in the NFL with his strength, hustle, and savvy.

Offensive Guard
TYRONE McGRIFF
6-0, 267
Pittsburgh Steelers

Tyrone McGriff (wow! what a name!) made history even before he was picked for the All-Rookie team. He was the 333rd and last man picked in the 1980 draft. The last man picked—and still made the All-Rookie team! Imagine! That, too, is now history. Oh, one more distinction: he is the shortest and widest guard in the NFL. McGriff was a three-time little All-American at Florida A&M, before being drafted (almost as a joke) by the Steelers. But after signing he decided he'd be better off playing in the Canadian League, with Hamilton—but was cut after a week. He asked the Steelers for another chance and they said, why not? Ty McGriff came to camp and stunned everyone with his strength and explosive blocking charge. When injuries sidelined a veteran starter, McGriff got his chance and by mid-October was a starter. "Don't call him 'lucky,'" says Coach Chuck Noll. "We're the lucky ones. A 333rd draft choice giving us offensive line strength. Pinch me, somebody. I can't believe it." But Tyrone McGriff believes it.

Center
TOM GINN
6-3, 255
Detroit Lions

One of the most difficult adjustments for a rookie is from playing center in college to playing center with the pros. The passing game in the pros is so much more complex and there are so many things  a center has to learn in helping to protect the QB. Tommy Ginn, who captained the Arkansas Razorbacks in college, was only a fifth-round draft choice, but from almost Day One in camp, the Detroit coaches were impressed with his hustle, his intelligence, and his quickness. A pretty good base to bring out the potential in a pro center, and Ginn responded to Lion coaching. "A lot of rookie centers can't take the head-slapping they get from defensive tackles," says Lion Coach, Monte Clark, "but Tommy takes it all and still makes his block." By mid-season, Ginn, as a starter, had already gained a lot of respect throughout the NFL. A real team player, Ginn shows it with the following statement: "First, I'd like to see the Lions make it to the playoffs—and then I'd like too make All-Pro." Tommy Ginn has his head on straight.

Quarterback
DAVID WOODLEY
6-2, 183
Miami Dolphins

Age had been creeping up on the great Bob Griese. So Coach Don Shula of the Dolphins decided to take a chance on the nifty rookie who'd looked so good in pre-season camp. David Woodley had only been an eight-round, 224th-player draft choice—which isn't very hopeful for QBs in the NFL—but there was something about his quiet intensity and his alertness that impressed the Dolphin coaches. They also noted his quick release and rifle arm. Midway through the season when Woodley put on a five-touchdown show against the Los Angeles Rams (three by passing, two running) the NFL was on notice: this kid was a comer. At Louisiana State he was a pinpoint passer and a dangerous scrambler when he decided to tote the ball (rushing for eight TDs, by the way). He was also taking a tough academic course in computer science. His computer mind helped shape him as a pro. As the Miami QB he recorded 1,850 yards on 176 on 327 attempts for a nifty 53.8 percent.

Running Back
BILLY SIMS
6-0, 210
Detroit Lions

Most scouts simply said he'd be the next superstar running back in the NFL. That he'd be as sensational as O.J. Simpson, Earl Campbell, and Tony Dorsett as a rookie. At Oklahoma he'd been All-America two straight years, rushing for 1,762 yards as a junior and 1,506 as a senior. He was a shoo-in for the Heisman Trophy. So, how long did it take for the Lions (who had first pick in the league) to make their first draft choice? They set a record with two-tenths of a second. The Lions found out in camp that Billy Sims had exactly the gifts they'd seen on Oklahoma films: great leg drive, tremendous acceleration from the first step, and flashing speed—plus awesome power. Guess who the Lions had installed at running back the first day of practice? Sims was just as good once the All-Out NFL War began. NFL defenders were prepared for him, but readiness doesn't put a halter on Billy Sims. He carried 313 times, slashed for 1,303 yards and scored 16 TDs. All-Pro in a year or two?

Running Back
JOE CRIBBS
5-11, 190
Buffalo Bills

The Bills knew Joe Cribbs wasn't very big, but they knew he was all heart and all effort. They liked what he did at Auburn and hoped he'd still be available on the second round of the draft. That's where the Bills grabbed him and everyone among the Bills' officials let go with a silent "whoopee!" You see, Cribbs was nothing short of sensational at Auburn. He rushed for 3,368 yards, an Auburn record and third highest in Southeast Conference history. The Bills knew he could take punishment (to go with his speed) because he rarely fumbled. He once carried the ball 288 straight times without a bobble. Cribbs had 37 career TDs at Auburn and was also the Tigers' top punt returner. Shortly into the Bills' pre-season camp, the coaches knew he'd have to be a starter—if not immediately, then eventually, before the season got too old. Cribbs quickly showed explosive speed and ability to slip through the narrowest crack — reminding Bills' fans of O.J. Simpson.

ALL-ROOKIE
DEFENSE
1980

E: **Rulon Jones,** Denver Broncos
E: **Jacob Green,** Seattle Seahawks
T: **Rush Brown,** St. Louis Cardinals
T: **Jim Stuckey,** San Francisco 49ers
LB: **Buddy Curry,** Atlanta Falcons
LB: **Al Richardson,** Atlanta Falcons
LB: **Bobby Leopold,** San Francisco 49ers
CB: **Don McNeal,** Miami Dolphins
CB: **Johnnie Johnson,** Los Angeles Rams
S: **Roynell Young,** Philadelphia Eagles
S: **Darrol Ray,** New York Jets

Defensive End
RULON JONES
6-6, 260
Denver Broncos

Rulon Jones's hobbies are a clue to his personality and his approach to football. Jones likes to hunt and fish—making him a natural predator, which is the way he plays football. The Bronco scouts looked at some game films of Jones playing for Utah State and in one contest they saw him make 15 solo tackles and three quarterback sacks. They noted his size and speed and added a written comment: "Let's grab this guy, quick." So the Broncs made him their first pick in the draft. Jones's performance in pre-season camp proved that no mistake had been made. The big rookie had a nose for the ball and a lot of hate for whoever was running with it. He was intelligent and very coachable. Everything carried over into the regular season and the word quickly got around the NFL. Nobody was going to fool this big kid and he was tough to block. The unseen label got pinned to him very quickly: FUTURE ALL-PRO.

Defensive End
JACOB GREEN
6-3, 247
Seattle Seahawks

When Seattle coaches and scouts looked at Jacob Green's college stats they wondered if he was for real. As an All-America at Texas A&M, he finished his career with 283 tackles, including 38 quarterback sacks. He also forced 12 fumbles. Now if he could only bring that ferocity into the pros. In order to find out, they knew they'd have to make him a first-round draft choice, because Jake Green wouldn't last long in the selection proceedings. The Seahawks didn't have to wait long to find out if Green could make the adjustment to NFL standards. He turned out to be just as fierce a rusher against the pros as he'd been in college. He had great mobility and hand-strength in fighting off the blockers. He was seldom fooled by a fake. What Jake Green had was all the tools needed for great defensive end play in the NFL.

Defensive Tackle
RUSH BROWN
6-2, 257
St. Louis Cardinals

It's doubtful if anyone had a more interesting path to pro stardom. His high school in North Carolina didn't even play football. Brown never even watched a game on TV, but when he joined the Air Force after graduation and was sent to Europe, he decided to go out for the team at his base—and was named Player of the Year in the U.S. Air Force League in 1975. A professor from Ball State, in Indiana, who was on duty in Europe, recruited Brown for the Ball State Cardinals, where Brown was eventually co-captain and made All-Mid America Conference. He acquired the nickname "Crush," because of his bruising tackles. From Ball State Cardinals to St. Louis Cardinals was his next step, even though it was a far-down 10th-round draft pick that took him there. Cardinal coaches had liked what he did in college but there weren't many 6-2 defensive tackles in the NFL, where 6-4 or 6-5 was the norm. But when the final cuts were made in training camp, Rush Brown was not only still around but very important in the Cards' plans.

Defensive Tackle
JIM STUCKEY
6-4, 251
San Francisco 49ers

At Clemson, Jim Stuckey was an All-America defensive end, but the 49ers weren't quite sure where they wanted to use him. All they were sure of was that they wanted him, badly, as a first round draftee, and they'd see later on where he'd best fit in. At Clemson, Stuckey was a far-ranging head-hunter, who had been a starter ever since his freshman year. He racked up 267 career tackles and had 28 tackles for losses. Rarely did the enemy ever turn his corner and they never ran over him. Nobody could block him one-on-one. The Falcons knew all this but they were pretty well set at defensive end. Then one of the coaches, observing him closely in camp, said Stuckey reminded him of Randy White, the Dallas Cowboys' great defensive tackle. Stuckey was the same size to the inch and pound and had the same slashing traits. The Falcons moved him to tackle before the regular season started, and the curly-haired blond fitted in as though he were born to play defensive tackle in the NFL. He was almost a unanimous choice for All-Rookie.

Linebacker
BUDDY CURRY
6-3, 221
Atlanta Falcons

Quick—when was the last time a team in the NFL placed two linebackers on the All-Rookie team? Answer: never before, until the Falcons did it this past season. Buddy Curry was one; Al Richardson was the other. And for good measure, Jim Laughlin, another rookie, was a strong back-up performer. How's that for youthful defense? At North Carolina, Curry was not only an honorable mention All-America but he was also an all-conference academic selection. He carried his classroom smarts onto the football field, and the Atlanta scouts could see it in his game films. What he brought with him to the Falcons as a second-round draft pick was excellent speed, great range, and a nose for the ball. It all translated out to toughness against the run and plenty of vigil against the pass. By the time pre-season camp was finished, the Falcons were sure he'd be a starter, and their fans backed it all up with signs which read: WELCOME TO THE NFL, BUDDY!

Linebacker
AL RICHARDSON
6-2, 206
ATLANTA FALCONS

Al Richardson wasn't drafted by the Falcons until the eighth round. But that was deceiving as far as his ability was concerned. The second of the Falcons' all-rookie linebacker selections had been operated on for a severe knee injury in 1975 at Georgia Tech and sat out all of 1976. He played very little in 1977, so all the Falcon scouts had to go on was his performance in his last two seasons. But he made so many tackles and batted down so many passes in two years that Atlanta coaches kept feeling tempted. When Richardson was still available by the eighth round, they went for him. His knee held up in camp and the pre-season exhibition games. Richardson was not only sound but positively brilliant by the time the NFL campaign began. Although he weighed only 206, opposing players claimed he played like 230, tough, hard-nosed, and a slasher who could fight his way to the ballcarrier. Enemy coaches hate the thought of Richardson putting on 15 more pounds—as he probably will.

Linebacker
BOBBY LEOPOLD
6-1, 215
SAN FRANCISCO 49ERS

The 49ers had a major problem as they went into the college draft last year. They had to improve their defense. So they drafted three linebackers. In the eighth round somebody on the 49er staff said, "Let's take another linebacker." Round eight is pretty far down the talent list but the 49ers took Bobby Leopold of Notre Dame. Leopold had rarely made the headlines with the Irish. The fans barely noticed him among the usual number of Irish stars. But the four-year letterman had been a solid performer, with 180 career tackles. "He's too small," the 49ers were warned, but a 49er coach remembered the old crack: "It's not the size of the dog that counts in a fight; it's the size of the fight in the dog." The 49ers took Leopold to camp and a lot of critics predicted he wouldn't be around when the season started. But the other NFL clubs knew he was around . . . and around . . . and around. Bobby Leopold was everywhere the action was, sniffing out the ballcarrier, hitting, breaking up the short passes. A little guy who plays big.

67

Cornerback
DON McNEAL
5-11½, 190
MIAMI DOLPHINS

Don McNeal never played football until his junior year in high school—and his ears were bleeding after his first practice. He didn't know he was supposed to put ear pads inside his helmet. Don  McNeal learned quickly after that—and was an All-America at Alabama. There he gained a reputation that all pro scouts like to hear: that of a "hitter." His toughness, combined with blazing speed, led to a first-round draft selection by the Dolphins, who figured he'd get some good experience as a rookie and maybe a starter in his second season. McNeal advanced the schedule by a full year and started as a rookie. "He covers pass receivers closer than their shadow," says Tom Keane, defensive back-field coach. "And when he hits 'em if they make a reception, they don't make a single yard after the hit. We think Don will be an All-Pro candidate any year, now."

Cornerback
JOHNNIE JOHNSON
6-1, 185
LOS ANGELES RAMS

There was so much that the Rams' scouts liked about Johnnie Johnson as they got ready for the 1980 draft that they thought they might be going overboard on him. The University of Texas All-America did everything just about perfectly. Now, if he could just transport all that talent to the NFL. At Texas, he was a vicious tackler against the run and covered pass receivers like a blanket. He also had great ability to read offensive patterns and could decide in a flash how the play would develop. Meanwhile, the Longhorns also used Johnson as a punt returner and he had a career mark of 114 returns for 1,104 yards. What he added up to was a PLAYER, as they like to say in the NFL. So the Rams went along with their scouts' judgment and made Johnson a number one draft choice. He didn't disappoint anyone. He made a rapid adjustment to the pro game and as a starter in the Rams' secondary he made believers out of every coach and opposing player in the NFL.

Safety
ROYNELL YOUNG
6-1, 181
PHILADELPHIA EAGLES

Roynell Young made a little history the very moment he signed on with the Eagles. He was the first defensive back the Eagles had ever selected in the first round of the NFL draft. Even with so many of the so-called "skill" positions to consider, the Eagles knew what they were doing when they went for a defensive back. They knew that Roynell Young was a soft-spoken, mild-mannered young man who enjoys reading the Bible and listening to gospel music. But they also knew his nickname in college was "Silent Storm" and for good reason. At little Alcorn State in Louisiana (the only college to offer him a scholarship), Young quickly became a hurricane in the Alcorn secondary: a deadly tackler and an eagle-eyed predator against the pass. Eagle scouts, checking his game films, did a lot of silent ooohing and ahhing and projected him as a safety. And it was as a head-cracking safety who could handle the big, tough NFL tight ends that Roynell Young made his mark.

Safety
DARROL RAY
6-1, 206
NEW YORK JETS

When the Jets took Darrol Ray in the second round of the 1980 draft, he came to them with the reputation that "he's wherever the football is." That was what he was noted for as the star of the University of Oklahoma defensive backfield. As a four-year starter for the Sooners he roamed his safety position like a center fielder, intercepting or batting down passes, coming up quickly to nail ball-carriers at the line of scrimmage, and creaming any receiver who dared catch the ball near him. Jet coaches figured he'd be a strong back-up for one of their veteran starters, but Darrol Ray had other ideas. From his first pre-season scrimmage he was an instant starter and head-hunter. Enemy QBs who thought they could pick on the rookie quickly discovered he had the reflexes and reactions of a veteran. Ray was all over the field just as the Jets' scouts predicted he'd be. Rarely was he fooled by opposing play-action. Never did a receiver get behind him to make the catch. Darrol Ray had given notice: a star is on the rise.

71

1980 FINAL STANDINGS
AMERICAN FOOTBALL
CONFERENCE

EASTERN DIVISION

	W	L	T	Pct.	Pts.	OP
*Buffalo	11	5	0	.688	320	260
New England	10	6	0	.625	441	325
Miami	8	8	0	.500	266	305
Baltimore	7	9	0	.438	355	387
N.Y. Jets	4	12	0	.250	302	395

CENTRAL DIVISION

	W	L	T	Pct.	Pts.	OP
*Cleveland	11	5	0	.688	357	310
#Houston	11	5	0	.688	295	251
Pittsburgh	9	7	0	.563	352	313
Cincinnati	6	10	0	.375	244	312

WESTERN DIVISION

	W	L	T	Pct.	Pts.	OP
*San Diego	11	5	0	.688	418	327
#Oakland	11	5	0	.688	364	306
Kansas City	8	8	0	.500	319	336
Denver	8	8	0	.500	310	323
Seattle	4	12	0	.250	291	408

*Division Champion; #Wild Card for playoffs

Note: Cleveland won AFC Central title because of better conference record than Houston (8-4 to 7-5). San Diego won AFC Western title over Oakland on basis of best net points in division games (plus 60 to plus 37).

AFC PLAYOFFS
AFC First Round
Oakland 27, Houston 7

Divisional Playoffs
San Diego 20, Buffalo 14
Oakland 14, Cleveland 12

Championship Game
Oakland 34, San Diego 27

Super Bowl XV
Oakland 27, Philadelphia 10

. . . And Previews for 1981

EASTERN DIVISION

New England Patriots

Tim Fox . . . Quick, tough operator at defensive back.

QUARTERBACKING:	🏈 🏈 🏈 🏈
RUNNING:	🏈 🏈 🏈
RECEIVING:	🏈 🏈 🏈
OFFENSIVE LINE:	🏈 🏈 🏈
DEFENSE:	🏈 🏈 🏈 🏈

Miami Dolphins

Delvin Williams . . . A running back with speed and power.

QUARTERBACKING:	🏈 🏈 🏈 🏈
RUNNING:	🏈 🏈 🏈 🏈
RECEIVING:	🏈 🏈 🏈
OFFENSIVE LINE:	🏈 🏈 🏈
DEFENSE:	🏈 🏈 🏈

Baltimore Colts

Bert Jones . . . The QB can make or break the Colts' chances.

QUARTERBACKING: ⬤ ⬤ ⬤ ⬤
RUNNING: ⬤ ⬤
RECEIVING: ⬤ ⬤ ◖
OFFENSIVE LINE: ⬤ ⬤ ◖
DEFENSE: ⬤ ⬤ ⬤ ◖

Buffalo Bills

Reggie McKenzie . . . Few offensive guards can pull out as he does.

QUARTERBACKING: ⬤ ⬤ ⬤ ◖
RUNNING: ⬤ ⬤ ◖
RECEIVING: ⬤ ⬤ ◖
OFFENSIVE LINE: ⬤ ⬤ ◖
DEFENSE: ⬤ ⬤ ⬤

New York Jets

Marvin Powell . . . The OT is always up there for All-Pro consideration.

QUARTERBACKING: ●●●◖
RUNNING: ●●●◖
RECEIVING: ●●●●
OFFENSIVE LINE: ●●●◖
DEFENSE: ●●●◖

WESTERN DIVISION

San Diego Chargers

Louie Karcher . . . Perennial top choice as defensive tackle.

QUARTERBACKING: ●●●●●
RUNNING: ●●●●
RECEIVING: ●●●●●
OFFENSIVE LINE: ●●●●
DEFENSE: ●●●●

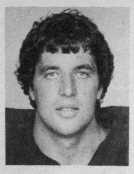

Oakland Raiders

Mark van Eeghen . . .
Most dependable of
Oakland's running backs.

QUARTERBACKING:	
RUNNING:	
RECEIVING:	
OFFENSIVE LINE:	
DEFENSE:	

Denver Broncos

Tom Glassic . . . Quick
offensive guard helps
running game go.

QUARTERBACKING:	
RUNNING:	
RECEIVING:	
OFFENSIVE LINE:	
DEFENSE:	

Seattle Seahawks

Dan Doornink . . . Main threat in Seattle's running game.

QUARTERBACKING:	🏈 🏈 🏈 🏈
RUNNING:	🏈 🏈 🏈 🏈
RECEIVING:	🏈 🏈 🏈 🏈
OFFENSIVE LINE:	🏈 🏈 🏈 🏈
DEFENSE:	🏈 🏈 🏈

Kansas City Chiefs

Gary Spani . . . One of the best all-around linebackers in NFL.

QUARTERBACKING:	🏈 🏈 🏈 🏈
RUNNING:	🏈 🏈 🏈 🏈
RECEIVING:	🏈 🏈 🏈 🏈
OFFENSIVE LINE:	🏈 🏈 🏈 🏈
DEFENSE:	🏈 🏈 🏈 🏈

Houston Oilers

Elvin Bethea . . . Leads the defensive charge from the tackle position.

QUARTERBACKING:	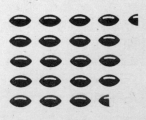
RUNNING:	
RECEIVING:	
OFFENSIVE LINE:	
DEFENSE:	

Cleveland Browns

Mike Pruitt . . . Main target for Brian Sipe's aerials.

QUARTERBACKING:	
RUNNING:	
RECEIVING:	
OFFENSIVE LINE:	
DEFENSE:	

Pittsburgh Steelers

Lynn Swann . . . Still one of the NFL's most dangerous wide receivers.

QUARTERBACKING:	●●●●◖
RUNNING:	●●●●
RECEIVING:	●●●●
OFFENSIVE LINE:	●●●◖
DEFENSE:	●●●●

Cincinnati Bengals

Pete Johnson . . . Huge fullback makes yards and catches passes.

QUARTERBACKING:	●●●◖
RUNNING:	●●●◖
RECEIVING:	●●●●
OFFENSIVE LINE:	●●●◖
DEFENSE:	●●●◖

1980 FINAL STANDINGS
NATIONAL FOOTBALL
CONFERENCE

EASTERN DIVISION

	W	L	T	Pct.	Pts.	OP
*Philadelphia	12	4	0	.750	384	222
#Dallas	12	4	0	.750	454	311
Washington	6	10	0	.375	261	293
St. Louis	5	11	0	.313	299	350
N.Y. Giants	4	12	0	.250	249	425

CENTRAL DIVISION

	W	L	T	Pct.	Pts.	OP
*Minnesota	9	7	0	.563	317	308
Detroit	9	7	0	.563	334	272
Chicago	7	9	0	.438	304	264
Tampa Bay	5	10	1	.344	231	371
Green Bay	5	10	1	.344	271	341

WESTERN DIVISION

	W	L	T	Pct.	Pts.	OP
*Atlanta	12	4	0	.750	405	272
#Los Angeles	11	5	0	.688	424	289
San Francisco	6	10	0	.375	320	415
New Orleans	1	15	0	.063	291	487

*Division Champion; #Wild Card for playoffs

Note: Philadelphia won NFC Eastern title over Dallas on basis of best net points in division games (plus 84 net points to plus 50). Minnesota won NFC Central title because of better conference record than Detroit (8-4 to 7-5).

NFC PLAYOFFS
NFC First Round
Dallas 34, Los Angeles 13
Divisional Playoffs
Philadelphia 31, Minnesota 16
Dallas 30, Atlanta 27
Championship Game
Philadelphia 20, Dallas 7
Super Bowl XV
Oakland 27, Philadelphia 10

. . . And Previews for 1981

EASTERN DIVISION

Philadelphia Eagles

Wilbert Montgomery . . .
One of NFL's most
dangerous running backs.

QUARTERBACKING: 🏈 🏈 🏈 🏈
RUNNING: 🏈 🏈 🏈 🏈
RECEIVING: 🏈 🏈 🏈 🏈
OFFENSIVE LINE: 🏈 🏈 🏈 🏈
DEFENSE: 🏈 🏈 🏈 🏈

Dallas Cowboys

Ed (Too Tall) Jones . . .
Gave up boxing and is
again top defensive end.

QUARTERBACKING: 🏈 🏈 🏈 🏈
RUNNING: 🏈 🏈 🏈 🏈
RECEIVING: 🏈 🏈 🏈 🏈
OFFENSIVE LINE: 🏈 🏈 🏈 🏈
DEFENSE: 🏈 🏈 🏈 🏈

81

St. Louis Cardinals

Dan Dierdorf . . . Still one of NFL's best offensive tackles.

QUARTERBACKING:	
RUNNING:	
RECEIVING:	
OFFENSIVE LINE:	
DEFENSE:	

Washington Redskins

Dave Butz . . . Giant defensive tackle anchors Skins up front.

QUARTERBACKING:
RUNNING:
RECEIVING:
OFFENSIVE LINE:
DEFENSE:

New York Giants

Gary Jeter . . . One of the league's toughest defensive ends.

QUARTERBACKING: ⬤ ⬤ ⬤
RUNNING: ⬤ ⬤ ⬤ ◖
RECEIVING: ⬤ ⬤ ⬤ ◖
OFFENSIVE LINE: ⬤ ⬤ ⬤ ⬤
DEFENSE: ⬤ ⬤ ⬤ ◖

WESTERN DIVISION

Atlanta Falcons

Steve Bartkowski . . . QB's rifle arm makes Birds a big threat.

QUARTERBACKING: ⬤ ⬤ ⬤ ⬤
RUNNING: ⬤ ⬤ ⬤
RECEIVING: ⬤ ⬤ ⬤
OFFENSIVE LINE: ⬤ ⬤ ⬤
DEFENSE: ⬤ ⬤ ⬤ ⬤

Los Angeles Rams

Doug France . . . His
blocking at OT helps
Rams' running attack.

QUARTERBACKING:	●	●	●	
RUNNING:	●	●	●	◖
RECEIVING:	●	●	●	●
OFFENSIVE LINE:	●	●	●	◖
DEFENSE:	●	●	●	●

San Francisco 49ers

Freddie Solomon . . .
Fleet receiver can make
the tough catches.

QUARTERBACKING:	●	●	●	◖
RUNNING:	●	●	●	◖
RECEIVING:	●	●	●	●
OFFENSIVE LINE:	●	●	●	◖
DEFENSE:	●	●	●	◖

New Orleans Saints

Tony Galbreath . . . Big running back makes the hard yards.

QUARTERBACKING:
RUNNING:
RECEIVING:
OFFENSIVE LINE:
DEFENSE:

CENTRAL DIVISION

Chicago Bears

Mike Hartenstine . . . Provides strong defensive strength at end.

QUARTERBACKING:
RUNNING:
RECEIVING:
OFFENSIVE LINE:
DEFENSE:

Detroit Lions

Gary Danielson . . . Gives Detroit excellent play at quarterback.

QUARTERBACKING: 🏈 🏈 🏈 🏈
RUNNING: 🏈 🏈 🏈 🏈
RECEIVING: 🏈 🏈 🏈 ◖
OFFENSIVE LINE: 🏈 🏈 🏈 ◖
DEFENSE: 🏈 🏈 🏈 ◖

Minnesota Vikings

Matt Blair . . . Dependable linebacker always in thick of things.

QUARTERBACKING: 🏈 🏈 🏈 ◖
RUNNING: 🏈 🏈 🏈 🏈
RECEIVING: 🏈 🏈 🏈 ◖
OFFENSIVE LINE: 🏈 🏈 🏈 ◖
DEFENSE: 🏈 🏈 🏈 🏈

Tampa Bay Buccaneers

Charley Hannah . . . Fine blocker and pass protector at OT.

QUARTERBACKING:
RUNNING:
RECEIVING:
OFFENSIVE LINE:
DEFENSE:

Green Bay Packers

Mark Koncar . . . Another OT who makes life easier for running backs.

QUARTERBACKING:
RUNNING:
RECEIVING:
OFFENSIVE LINE:
DEFENSE:

HOW THEY'RE PICKED
TO FINISH IN 1981

AFC

East
1. New England
2. Miami
3. Baltimore
4. Buffalo
5. New York Jets

West
1. San Diego
2. Oakland
3. Denver
4. Seattle
5. Kansas City

Central
1. Houston
2. Cleveland
3. Pittsburgh
4. Cincinnati

NFC

East
1. Philadelphia
2. Dallas
3. St. Louis
4. Washington
5. New York Giants

West
1. Atlanta
2. Los Angeles
3. San Francisco
4. New Orleans

Central
1. Chicago
2. Detroit
3. Minnesota
4. Tampa Bay
5. Green Bay

Super Bowl XVI
San Diego vs. Philadelphia

Best Bet for
Rookie of the Year
George Rogers of New Orleans Saints
or
Hugh Green of Tampa Bay Buccaneers

1980 RECORDS

SCORING

POINTS
Kickers
AFC: 129 John Smith, New England
NFC: 116 Ed Murray, Detroit
Non-kickers
NFC: 96 Billy Sims, Detroit
AFC: 78 Earl Campbell, Houston
Curtis Dickey, Baltimore
John Jefferson, San Diego

TOUCHDOWNS
NFC: 16 Billy Sims, Detroit (13 rushing, 3 receiving)
AFC: 13 Earl Campbell, Houston (13 rushing)
Curtis Dickey, Baltimore (11 rushing, 2 receiving)
John Jefferson, San Diego (13 receiving)

EXTRA POINTS
NFC: 59 Rafael Septien, Dallas (60 attempts)
AFC: 51 John Smith, New England (51 attempts)

FIELD GOALS
NFC: 27 Ed Murray, Detroit (42 attempts)
AFC: 26 John Smith, New England (34 attempts)
Fred Steinfort, Denver (34 attempts)

MOST POINTS, GAME
NFC: 24 points Earnest Gray, New York vs. St. Louis,
September 7 (4 TDs)
AFC: 18 points Jim Smith, Pittsburgh vs. Chicago,
September 28 (3 TDs)
Bob Chandler, Oakland vs. Seattle, October 26 (3 TDs)

TEAM LEADERS
AFC: BALTIMORE: 79, Steve Mike-Mayer; BUFFALO: 76, Nick
Mike-Mayer; CINCINNATI: 48, Ian Sunter; CLEVELAND: 87,
Don Cockroft; DENVER: 110, Fred Steinfort; HOUSTON: 83,
Toni Fritsch; KANSAS CITY: 97, Nick Lowery; MIAMI: 74,

Uwe von Schamann; NEW ENGLAND: 129, John Smith; NEW
YORK: 78, Pat Leahy; OAKLAND: 98, Chris Bahr;
PITTSBURGH: 96, Matt Bahr; SAN DIEGO: 118, Rolf
Benirschke; SEATTLE: 93, Efren Herrera.
NFC: ATLANTA: 103, Tim Mazzetti; CHICAGO: 74, Bob Thomas;
DALLAS: 92, Rafael Septien; DETROIT: 116, Ed Murray;
GREEN BAY: 48, Gerry Ellis; LOS ANGELES: 99, Frank Corral;
MINNESOTA: 81, Rick Danmeier; NEW ORLEANS: 61, Benny
Ricardo; NEW YORK: 75, Joe Danelo; PHILADELPHIA: 96,
Tony Franklin; ST. LOUIS: 54, Ottis Anderson; SAN
FRANCISCO: 78, Ray Wersching; TAMPA BAY: 79, Garo
Yepremian; WASHINGTON: 81, Mark Moseley.

TEAM CHAMPION

NFC: 454 Dallas
AFC: 441 New England

TOP TEN SCORERS—NON-KICKERS

	TD	R	P	M	PTS
Sims, Billy, Det.	16	13	3	0	96
Campbell, Earl, Hou.	13	13	0	0	78
Dickey, Curtis, Balt.	13	11	2	0	78
Jefferson, John, S.D.	13	0	13	0	78
Cribbs, Joe, Buff.	12	11	1	0	72
Dorsett, Tony, Dall.	11	11	0	0	66
Brown, Ted, Minn.	10	8	2	0	60
Chandler, Bob, Oak.	10	0	10	0	60
Gray, Earnest, N.Y.G.	10	0	10	0	60
Montgomery, Wilbert, Phil. .	10	8	2	0	60
Solomon, Freddie, S.F.	10	0	8	2	60

TOP TEN SCORERS—KICKERS

	XP	XPA	FG	FGA	PTS
Smith, John, N.E.	51	51	26	34	129
Benirschke, Rolf, S.D.	46	48	24	36	118
Murray, Ed, Det.	35	36	27	42	116
Steinfort, Fred, Den.	32	33	26	34	110

Mazzetti, Tim, Atl.	46	49	19	27	103
Corral, Frank, L.A.	51	52	16	30	99
Bahr, Chris, Oak.	41	44	19	37	98
Lowery, Nick, K.C.	37	37	20	26	97
Bahr, Matt, Pitt.	39	42	19	28	96
Franklin, Tony, Phil.	48	48	16	31	96

AFC—INDIVIDUAL

NON-KICKERS

	TD	R	P	M	PTS
Campbell, Earl, Hou.	13	13	0	0	78
Dickey, Curtis, Balt.	13	11	2	0	78
Jefferson, John, S.D.	13	0	13	0	78
Cribbs, Joe, Buff.	12	11	1	0	72
Chandler, Bob, Oak.	10	0	10	0	60
Calhoun, Don, N.E.	9	9	0	0	54
Smith, Jim, Pitt.	9	0	9	0	54
Winslow, Kellen, S.D.	9	0	9	0	54
Francis, Russ, N.E.	8	0	8	0	48
Branch, Cliff, Oak.	7	0	7	0	42
Dierking, Scott, N.Y.J.	7	6	1	0	42
Johnson, Pete, Cin.	7	6	1	0	42
Moore, Nat, Mia.	7	0	7	0	42
Swann, Lynn, Pitt.	7	0	7	0	42

NFC—INDIVIDUALS

NON-KICKERS

	TD	R	P	M	PTS
Sims, Billy, Det.	16	13	3	0	96
Dorsett, Tony, Dall.	11	11	0	0	66
Brown, Ted, Minn.	10	8	2	0	60
Gray, Earnest, N.Y.G.	10	0	10	0	60
Montgomery, Wilbert, Phil. .	10	8	2	0	60
Solomon, Freddie, S.F.	10	0	8	2	60

Anderson, Ottis, St.L.	9	9	0	0	54
Cain, Lynn, Atl.	9	8	1	0	54
Carmichael, Harold, Phil. . . .	9	0	9	0	54
Cooper, Earl, S.F.	9	5	4	0	54
Miller, Junior, Atl.	9	0	9	0	54
Peacock, Elvis, L.A.	9	7	2	0	54
Clark, Dwight, S.F.	8	0	8	0	48
Ellis, Gerry, G.B.	8	5	3	0	48
Evans, Vince, Chi.	8	8	0	0	48
Harmon, Clarence, Wash. . .	8	4	4	0	48
Hill, Tony, Dall.	8	0	8	0	48
Miller, Willie, L.A.	8	0	8	0	48

RUSHING

YARDS
AFC: 1934 Earl Campbell, Houston
NFC: 1460 Walter Payton, Chicago

YARDS PER ATTEMPT
AFC: 5.2 Earl Campbell, Houston
NFC: 5.0 Dexter Bussey, Detroit

TOUCHDOWNS
AFC: 13 Earl Campbell, Houston
NFC: 13 Billy Sims, Detroit

ATTEMPTS
AFC: 373 Earl Campbell, Houston
NFC: 317 Walter Payton, Chicago

LONGEST
AFC: 89 yards Kenny King, Oakland vs. San Diego, October 12 (TD)
NFC: 72 yards Wilbert Montgomery, Philadelphia vs. Minnesota, September 14 (TD)

MOST YARDS, GAME

AFC: 206 yards (31 attempts) Earl Campbell, Houston vs. Chicago, November 16

NFC: 183 yards (18 attempts) Walter Payton, Chichago vs. New Orleans, September 14

183 yards (24 attempts) Tony Dorsett, Dallas vs. New York Giants, November 9

TEAM LEADERS

AFC: BALTIMORE: 800, Curtis Dickey; BUFFALO: 1185, Joe Cribbs; CINCINNATI: 747, Pete Johnson; CLEVELAND: 1034, Mike Pruitt; DENVER: 476, Jim Jensen; HOUSTON: 1934, Earl Campbell; KANSAS CITY: 693, Ted McKnight; MIAMI: 671, Delvin Williams; NEW ENGLAND: 818, Vagas Ferguson; NEW YORK: 567, Scott Dierking; OAKLAND: 838, Mark van Eeghen; PITTSBURGH: 789, Franco Harris; SAN DIEGO: 827, Chuck Muncie; SEATTLE: 632, Jim Jodat.

NFC: ATLANTA: 1308, William Andrews; CHICAGO: 1460, Walter Payton; DALLAS: 1185, Tony Dorsett; DETROIT: 1303, Billy Sims; GREEN BAY: 831, Eddie Lee Ivery; LOS ANGELES: 807, Cullen Bryant; MINNESOTA: 912, Ted Brown; NEW ORLEANS: 366, Jimmy Rogers; NEW YORK: 580, Billy Taylor; PHILADELPHIA: 778, Wilbert Montgomery; ST. LOUIS: 1352, Ottis Anderson; SAN FRANCISCO: 720, Earl Cooper; TAMPA BAY: 599, Ricky Bell; WASHINGTON: 708, Wilbur Jackson.

TEAM CHAMPION

NFC: 2799 Los Angeles
AFC: 2635 Houston

TOP TEN RUSHERS

	Att	Yards	Avg	Long	TD
Campbell, Earl, Hou.	373	1934	5.2	t55	13
Payton, Walter, Chi.	317	1460	4.6	t69	6
Anderson, Ottis, St.L.	301	1352	4.5	52	9
Andrews, William, Atl.	265	1308	4.9	33	4
Sims, Billy, Det.	313	1303	4.2	52	13
Dorsett, Tony, Dall.	278	1185	4.3	56	11
Cribbs, Joe, Buff.	306	1185	3.9	48	11

	Att	Yards	Avg	Long	TD
Pruitt, Mike, Clev.	249	1034	4.2	t56	6
Cain, Lynn, Atl.	235	914	3.9	37	8
Brown, Ted, Minn.	219	912	4.2	t55	8

AFC—INDIVIDUALS

	Att	Yards	Avg	Long	TD
Campbell, Earl, Hou.	373	1934	5.2	t55	13
Cribbs, Joe, Buff.	306	1185	3.9	48	11
Pruitt, Mike, Clev.	249	1034	4.2	t56	6
van Eeghen, Mark, Oak. . . .	222	838	3.8	34	5
Muncie, Chuck, N.O.-S.D. . . .	175	827	4.7	53	6
Ferguson, Vagas, N.E.	211	818	3.9	44	2
Dickey, Curtis, Balt.	176	800	4.5	t51	11
Harris, Franco, Pitt.	208	789	3.8	26	4
Calhoun, Don, N.E.	200	787	3.9	t22	9
King, Kenny, Oak.	172	761	4.4	t89	4
Johnson, Pete, Cin.	186	747	4.0	t57	6
Alexander, Charles, Cin. . . .	169	702	4.2	37	2
McKnight, Ted, K.C.	206	693	3.4	25	3
Williams, Delvin, Mia.	187	671	3.6	65	2
Jodat, Jim, Sea.	155	632	4.1	26	5

NFC—INDIVIDUALS

	Att	Yards	Avg	Long	TD
Payton, Walter, Chi.	317	1460	4.6	t69	6
Anderson, Ottis, St.L.	301	1352	4.5	52	9
Andrews, William, Atl.	265	1308	4.9	33	4
Sims, Billy, Det.	313	1303	4.2	52	13
Dorsett, Tony, Dall.	278	1185	4.3	56	11
Cain, Lynn, Atl.	235	914	3.9	37	8
Brown, Ted, Minn.	219	912	4.2	t55	8
Ivery, Eddie Lee, G.B.	202	831	4.1	t38	3
Bryant, Cullen, L.A.	183	807	4.4	20	3
Montgomery, Wilbert, Phil. .	193	778	4.0	t72	8
Peacock, Elvis, L.A.	164	777	4.7	36	7
Bussey, Dexter, Det.	145	720	5.0	40	3

Cooper, Earl, S.F.	171	720	4.2	47	5
Jackson, Wilbur, Wash. ...	176	708	4.0	t55	3
Bell, Ricky, T.B.	174	599	3.4	40	2

PASSING

HIGHEST RATING
AFC: 91.4 Brian Sipe, Cleveland
NFC: 90.9 Ron Jaworski, Philadelphia

ATTEMPTS
AFC: 589 Dan Fouts, San Diego
NFC: 522 Tommy Kramer, Minnesota

COMPLETIONS
AFC: 348 Dan Fouts, San Diego
NFC: 309 Archie Manning, New Orleans

COMPLETION PERCENTAGE
NFC: 64.5 Joe Montana, San Francisco (273 attempts, 176 completions)
AFC: 64.1 Ken Stabler, Houston (457 attempts, 293 completions)

YARDS
AFC: 4715 Dan Fouts, San Diego
NFC: 3716 Archie Manning, New Orleans

TOUCHDOWN PASSES
NFC: 31 Steve Bartkowski, Atlanta
AFC: 30 Dan Fouts, San Diego
        Brian Sipe, Cleveland

INTERCEPTIONS
AFC: 30 Richard Todd, New York
NFC: 25 Lynn Dickey, Green Bay
        Danny White, Dallas

LOWEST PERCENTAGE INTERCEPTED
AFC: 2.5   Brian Sipe, Cleveland (554 attempts, 14 intercepted)
NFC: 2.6   Gary Danielson, Detroit (417 attempts, 11 intercepted)

TEAM CHAMPION
NFC: 92.4   Philadelphia
AFC: 91.4   Cleveland

TOP TEN INDIVIDUAL PASSING QUALIFIERS

	Att	Comp	Yards	TD	Int	Rating Points
Sipe, Brian, Clev.	554	337	4132	30	14	91.4
Jaworski, Ron, Phil.	451	257	3529	27	12	90.9
Ferragamo, Vince, L.A.	404	240	3199	30	19	89.7
Bartkowski, Steve, Atl.	463	257	3544	31	16	88.0
Montana, Joe, S.F.	273	176	1795	15	9	87.8
Fouts, Dan, S.D.	589	348	4715	30	24	84.6
Danielson, Gary, Det.	417	244	3223	13	11	82.6
Manning, Archie, N.O.	509	309	3716	23	20	81.8
White, Danny, Dall.	436	260	3287	28	25	80.8
Morton, Craig, Den.	301	183	2150	12	13	77.9

AFC INDIVIDUAL QUALIFIERS

	Att	Comp	Yards	TD	Int	Rating Points
Sipe, Brian, Clev.	554	337	4132	30	14	91.4
Fouts, Dan, S.D.	589	348	4715	30	24	84.6
Morton, Craig, Den.	301	183	2150	12	13	77.9
Fuller, Steve, K.C.	320	193	2250	10	12	76.1
Jones, Bert, Balt.	446	248	3134	23	21	75.5
Bradshaw, Terry, Pitt.	424	218	3339	24	22	75.1
Ferguson, Joe, Buff.	439	251	2805	20	18	74.6
Grogan, Steve, N.E.	306	175	2475	18	22	73.1
Plunkett, Jim, Oak.	320	165	2299	18	16	72.8
Zorn, Jim, Sea.	488	276	3346	17	20	72.4
Stabler, Ken, Hou.	457	293	3202	13	28	68.6
Anderson, Ken, Cin.	275	166	1778	6	13	67.1

	Att	Comp	Yards	TD	Int	Rating Points
Woodley, David, Mia. . . .	327	176	1850	14	17	63.2
Todd, Richard, N.Y.J. . . .	479	264	3329	17	30	62.4
Thompson, Jack, Cin. . . .	234	115	1324	11	12	61.0

NFC INDIVIDUAL QUALIFIERS

	Att	Comp	Yards	TD	Int	Rating Points
Jaworski, Ron, Phil.	451	257	3529	27	12	90.9
Ferragamo, Vince, L.A. . .	404	240	3199	30	19	89.7
Bartkowski, Steve, Atl. . .	463	257	3544	31	16	88.0
Montana, Joe, S.F.	273	176	1795	15	9	87.8
Danielson, Gary, Det. . . .	417	244	3223	13	11	82.6
Manning, Archie, N.O. . .	509	309	3716	23	20	81.8
White, Danny, Dall.	436	260	3287	28	25	80.8
Theismann, Joe, Wash. . .	454	262	2962	17	16	75.1
Kramer, Tommy, Minn. . .	522	299	3582	19	23	72.1
Dickey, Lynn, G.B.	478	278	3529	15	25	70.0
Williams, Doug, T.B. . . .	521	254	3396	20	16	69.7
Hart, Jim, St.L.	425	228	2946	16	20	68.7
DeBerg, Steve, S.F.	321	186	1998	12	17	66.5
Evans, Vince, Chi.	278	148	2039	11	16	66.1
Simms, Phil, N.Y.G. . . .	402	193	2321	15	19	58.9

PASS RECEIVING

RECEPTIONS
AFC: 89 Kellen Winslow, San Diego
NFC: 83 Earl Cooper, San Francisco

YARDS
AFC: 1340 John Jefferson, San Diego
NFC: 1226 James Lofton, Green Bay

YARDS PER RECEPTION
AFC: 22.0 Stanley Morgan, New England
NFC: 19.3 James Scott, Chicago

TOUCHDOWNS
AFC: 13   John Jefferson, San Diego
NFC: 10   Earnest Gray, New York

LONGEST
NFC: 93 yards   Freddie Solomon, San Francisco vs. Atlanta, September 28 (from Steve DeBerg)—TD
AFC: 86 yards   Cliff Branch, Oakland vs. Philadelphia, November 23 (from Jim Plunkett)—TD

MOST RECEPTIONS, GAME
AFC: 17 (160 yards)   Clark Gaines, New York vs. San Francisco, September 21
NFC: 12 (118 yards)   Clarence Harmon, Washington vs. San Diego, December 7

TEAM LEADERS
AFC: BALTIMORE: 61, Roger Carr; BUFFALO: 57, Jerry Butler; CINCINNATI: 56, Dan Ross; CLEVELAND: 63, Mike Pruitt; DENVER: 49, Jim Jensen; HOUSTON: 59, Mike Barber; KANSAS CITY: 47, Henry Marshall; MIAMI: 57, Tony Nathan; NEW ENGLAND: 45, Stanley Morgan; NEW YORK: 50, Bruce Harper; OAKLAND: 49, Bob Chandler; PITTSBURGH: 44, Lynn Swann; SAN DIEGO: 89, Kellen Winslow; SEATTLE: 66, Steve Largent.
NFC: ATLANTA: 57, Alfred Jenkins; CHICAGO: 46, Walter Payton; DALLAS: 60, Tony Hill; DETROIT: 53, Freddie Scott; GREEN BAY: 71, James Lofton; LOS ANGELES: 53, Cullen Bryant; MINNESOTA: 69, Ahmad Rashad; NEW ORLEANS: 65, Wes Chandler; NEW YORK: 52, Earnest Gray; 50, Wilbert Montgomery; ST. LOUIS: 68, Pat Tilley; SAN FRANCISCO: 83, Earl Cooper; TAMPA BAY: 48, Gordon Jones; WASHINGTON: 58, Art Monk.

TOP TEN PASS RECEIVERS

	No	Yards	Avg	Long	TD
Winslow, Kellen, S.D.	89	1290	14.5	65	9
Cooper, Earl, S.F.	83	567	6.8	t66	4
Jefferson, John, S.D.	82	1340	16.3	t58	13
Clark, Dwight, S.F.	82	991	12.1	t71	8

	No	Yards	Avg	Long	TD
Lofton, James, G.B.	71	1226	17.3	47	4
Joiner, Charlie, S.D.	71	1132	15.9	51	4
Rashad, Ahmad, Minn.	69	1095	15.9	t76	5
Tilley, Pat, St.L.	68	966	14.2	t60	6
Largent, Steve, Sea.	66	1064	16.1	t67	6
Chandler, Wes, N.O.	65	975	15.0	50	6

AFC—INDIVIDUALS

	No	Yards	Avg	Long	TD
Winslow, Kellen, S.D.	89	1290	14.5	65	9
Jefferson, John, S.D.	82	1340	16.3	t58	13
Joiner, Charlie, S.D.	71	1132	15.9	51	4
Largent, Steve, Sea.	66	1064	16.1	t67	6
Pruitt, Mike, Clev.	63	471	7.5	28	0
McCullum, Sam, Sea.	62	874	14.1	58	6
Carr, Roger, Balt.	61	924	15.1	43	5
Barber, Mike, Hou.	59	712	12.1	t79	5
Butler, Jerry, Buff.	57	832	14.6	69	6
Nathan, Tony, Mia.	57	588	10.3	61	5
Casper, Dave, Oak.-Hou.	56	796	14.2	43	4
Ross, Dan, Cin.	56	724	12.9	37	4
Rucker, Reggie, Clev.	52	768	14.8	45	4
Cribbs, Joe, Buff.	52	415	8.0	t21	1
Logan, Dave, Clev.	51	822	16.1	65	4

NFC—INDIVIDUALS

	No	Yards	Avg	Long	Td
Cooper, Earl, S.F.	83	567	6.8	t66	4
Clark, Dwight, S.F.	82	991	12.1	t71	8
Lofton, James, G.B.	71	1226	17.3	47	4
Rashad, Ahmad, Minn.	69	1095	15.9	t76	5
Tilley, Pat, St.L.	68	966	14.2	t60	6
Chandler, Wes, N.O.	65	975	15.0	50	6
Young, Rickey, Minn.	64	499	7.8	22	2
Brown, Ted, Minn.	62	623	10.0	t67	2
Hill, Tony, Dall.	60	1055	17.6	t58	8
Monk, Art, Wash.	58	797	13.7	t54	3

Jenkins, Alfred, Atl.	57	1026	18.0	57	6
Galbreath, Tony, N.O.	57	470	8.2	21	2
Francis, Wallace, Atl.	54	862	16.0	t81	7
Harmon, Clarence, Wash.	54	534	9.9	45	4
White, Sammy, Minn.	53	887	16.7	50	5

INTERCEPTIONS

INTERCEPTIONS
AFC: 13 Lester Hayes, Oakland
NFC: 8 Nolan Cromwell, Los Angeles

YARDS
AFC: 273 Lester Hayes, Oakland
NFC: 140 Nolan Cromwell, Los Angeles

TOUCHDOWNS
AFC: 2 Ray Griffin, Cincinnati
NFC: 1 by many players

LONGEST
NFC: 99 yards Johnnie Johnson, Los Angeles vs. Green Bay, September 21 (TD)
AFC: 93 yards Randy Gradishar, Denver vs. Cleveland, October 5 (TD)

TEAM LEADERS
AFC: BALTIMORE: 5, Bruce Laird; BUFFALO: 7, Steve Freeman; CINCINNATI: 7, Louis Breeden; CLEVELAND: 6, Ron Bolton; DENVER: 4, Steve Foley; HOUSTON: 7, Jack Tatum; KANSAS CITY: 10, Gary Barbaro; MIAMI: 7, Gerald Small; NEW ENGLAND: 5, Ray Clayborn; NEW YORK: 8, Ken Schroy; OAKLAND: 13, Lester Hayes; PITTSBURGH: 7, Donnie Shell; SAN DIEGO: 5, Glen Edwards; SEATTLE: 6, Dave Brown & John Harris.

NFC: ATLANTA: 7, Al Richardson; CHICAGO: 4, Len Walterscheid; DALLAS: 5, Dennis Thurman & Charlie Waters; DETROIT: 6, Jimmy Allen & James Hunter; GREEN BAY: 5, Johnnie Gray; LOS ANGELES: 8, Nolan Cromwell;

MINNESOTA: 6, John Turner; NEW ORLEANS: 5, Tom Myers; NEW YORK: 5, Mike Dennis; PHILADELPHIA: 6, Brenard Wilson; ST. LOUIS: 5, Ken Stone; SAN FRANCISCO: 4, Ricky Churchman & Dwight Hicks; TAMPA BAY: 4, Mike Washington; WASHINGTON: 7, Lemar Parrish.

TEAM CHAMPION

AFC: 35 Oakland
NFC: 33 Washington

TOP TEN INTERCEPTORS

	No	Yards	Avg	Long	TD
Hayes, Lester, Oak.	13	273	21.0	62	1
Barbaro, Gary, K.C.	10	163	16.3	39	0
Cromwell, Nolan, L.A.	8	140	17.5	34	1
Schroy, Ken, N.Y.J.	8	91	11.4	t82	1
Richardson, Al, Atl.	7	139	19.9	52	0
Shell, Donnie, Pitt.	7	135	19.3	67	0
Freeman, Steve, Buff.	7	107	15.3	t47	1
Tatum, Jack, Hou.	7	100	14.3	35	0
Breeden, Louis, Cin.	7	91	13.0	29	0
Harris, Eric, K.C.	7	54	7.7	41	0
Small, Gerald, Mia.	7	46	6.6	22	0
Parrish, Lemar, Wash.	7	13	1.9	9	0

AFC—INDIVIDUALS

	No	Yards	Avg	Long	TD
Hayes, Lester, Oak.	13	273	21.0	62	1
Barbaro, Gary, K.C.	10	163	16.3	39	0
Schroy, Ken, N.Y.J.	8	91	11.4	t82	1
Shell, Donnie, Pitt.	7	135	19.3	67	0
Freeman, Steve, Buff.	7	107	15.3	t47	1
Tatum, Jack, Hou.	7	100	14.3	35	0
Breeden, Louis, Cin.	7	91	13.0	29	0
Harris, Eric, K.C.	7	54	7.7	41	0
Small, Gerald, Mia.	7	46	6.6	22	0
Ray, Darrol, N.Y.J.	6	132	22.0	t71	1

Bolton, Ron, Clev.	6	62	10.3	29	0
Brown, Dave, Sea.	6	32	5.3	24	0
Harris, John, Sea.	6	28	4.7	15	0
Wagner, Mike, Pitt.	6	27	4.5	17	0
Edwards, Glen, S.D.	5	122	24.4	t68	1
Clayborn, Ray, N.E.	5	87	17.4	29	0
Perry, Vernon, Hou.	5	85	17.0	42	0
Nixon, Jeff, Buff.	5	81	16.2	t50	1
Laird, Bruce, Balt.	5	71	14.2	18	0
Burrell, Clinton, Clev.	5	51	10.2	29	0
McNeal, Don, Mia.	5	17	3.4	15	0
Dykes, Donald, N.Y.J.	5	1	0.2	1	0

NFC—INDIVIDUALS

	No	Yards	Avg	Long	TD
Cromwell, Nolan, L.A.	8	140	17.5	34	1
Richardson, Al, Atl.	7	139	19.9	52	0
Parrish, Lemar, Wash.	7	13	1.9	9	0
Lavender, Joe, Wash.	6	96	16.0	t51	1
Wilson, Brenard, Phil.	6	79	13.2	41	0
Murphy, Mark, Wash.	6	58	9.7	28	0
Allen, Jimmy, Det.	6	38	6.3	23	0
Turner, John, Minn.	6	22	3.7	13	0
Hunter, James, Det.	6	20	3.3	13	0
Perry, Rod, L.A.	5	115	23.0	t83	1
Thurman, Dennis, Dall.	5	114	22.8	t78	1
Myers, Tom, N.O.	5	96	19.2	48	0
Waters, Charlie, Dall.	5	78	15.6	29	0
Dennis, Mike, N.Y.G.	5	68	13.6	28	0
Stone, Ken, St.L.	5	63	12.6	20	0
Gray, Johnnie, G.B.	5	54	10.8	21	0

PUNTING

YARDS PER PUNT
NFC: 44.8   Dave Jennings, New York (94 punts, 4211 yards)
AFC: 43.9   Luke Prestridge, Denver (70 punts, 3075 yards)

NET AVERAGE
NFC: 36.6   Dave Jennings, New York (94 total punts, 3445 yards)
AFC: 35.9   Ray Guy, Oakland (71 total punts, 2551 yards)

LONGEST
AFC: 71 yards   George Roberts, Miami vs. Oakland, November 2

NFC: 67 yards   Tom Skladany, Detroit vs. Minnesota, November 9

PUNTS
NFC: 99   Larry Swider, St. Louis
AFC: 84   Bob Grupp, Kansas City

Team Champion
NFC: 44.8   New York
AFC: 43.9   Denver

TOP TEN PUNTERS

	No	Yds	Long	Avg
Jennings, Dave, N.Y.G.	94	4211	63	44.8
Prestridge, Luke, Den.	70	3075	57	43.9
Guy, Ray, Oak.	71	3099	66	43.6
Roberts, George, Mia.	77	3279	71	42.6
Ramsey, Chuck, N.Y.J.	73	3096	59	42.4
Blanchard, Tom, T.B.	88	3722	62	42.3
Skladany, Tom, Det.	72	3036	67	42.2
Weaver, Herman, Sea.	67	2798	62	41.8
Swider, Larry, St.L.	99	4111	66	41.5
Miller, Jim, S.F.	77	3152	65	40.9

PUNT RETURNS

YARDS PER RETURN
AFC: 14.5   J.T. Smith, Kansas City (40 returns, 581 yards)
NFC: 12.2   Kenny Johnson, Atlanta (23 returns, 281 yards)

YARDS
AFC: 581   J.T. Smith, Kansas City
NFC: 548   James Jones, Dallas

RETURNS
NFC: 57   Danny Reece, Tampa Bay
AFC: 48   Ira Matthews, Oakland

LONGEST
AFC: 75 yards   Roland James, New England vs. New York Jets, November 2 (TD); Will Lewis, Seattle vs. Denver, November 23 (TD); J.T. Smith, Kansas City vs. St. Louis, November 23 (TD)
NFC: 66 yards   Alvin Garrett, New York vs St. Louis, September 7

TOUCHDOWNS
AFC: Roland James, New England vs. New York Jets, November 2 (75 yards); Will Lewis, Seattle vs. Denver, November 23 (75 yards); J.T. Smith, Kansas City vs. St. Louis, November 23 (75 yards); vs. Baltimore, December 21 (53 yards)
NFC: Roy Green, St. Louis vs. Detroit, December 7 (57 yards); Freddie Solomon, San Francisco vs. Tampa Bay, October 26 (53 yards); vs. New Orleans, December 7 (57 yards)

TEAM CHAMPION
AFC: 14.5   Kansas City (40 returns, 581 yards)
NFC: 10.1   Washington (48 returns, 487 yards)

TOP TEN PUNT RETURNERS

	No	FC	Yards	Avg	Long	TD
Smith, J. T., K.C.	40	8	581	14.5	t75	2
Johnson, Kenny, Atl. ..	23	5	281	12.2	56	0
Solomon, Freddie, S.F. .	27	2	298	11.0	t57	2
Green, Roy, St.L.	16	6	168	10.5	t57	1
Jones, James, Dall. ...	54	4	548	10.1	52	0
Nelms, Mike, Wash.	48	5	487	10.1	64	0
James, Roland, N.E. ..	33	3	331	10.0	t75	1

	No	FC	Yards	Avg	Long	TD
Bell, Theo, Pitt.	34	6	339	10.0	27	0
Fuller, Mike, S.D.	30	12	298	9.9	31	0
Smith, Reggie, Atl. ...	27	4	262	9.7	25	0

AFC—INDIVIDUALS

	No	FC	Yards	Avg	Long	TD
Smith, J.T., K.C.	40	8	581	14.5	t75	2
James, Roland, N.E. ..	33	3	331	10.0	t75	1
Bell, Theo, Pitt.	34	6	339	10.0	27	0
Fuller, Mike, S.D.	30	12	298	9.9	31	0
Upchurch, Rick, Den. ..	37	6	353	9.5	34	0
Matthews, Ira, Oak. ...	48	7	421	8.8	34	0
Harper, Bruce, N.Y.J. ..	28	7	242	8.6	24	0
Lewis, Will, Sea.	41	9	349	8.5	t75	1
Haynes, Mike, N.E. ...	17	2	140	8.2	35	0
Roaches, Carl, Hou. ...	47	6	384	8.2	68	0

NFC—INDIVIDUALS

	No	FC	Yards	Avg	Long	TD
Johnson, Kenny, Atl. ..	23	5	281	12.2	56	0
Solomon, Freddie, S.F. .	27	2	298	11.0	t57	2
Green, Roy, St.L.	16	6	168	10.5	t57	1
Jones, James, Dall. ...	54	4	548	10.1	52	0
Nelms, Mike, Wash. ...	48	5	487	10.1	64	0
Smith, Reggie, Atl. ...	27	4	262	9.7	25	0
Williams, Ray, Det. ...	27	4	259	9.6	53	0
Bell, Mark, St.L.	21	3	195	9.3	54	0
Sciarra, John, Phil. ...	36	1	330	9.2	32	0
Henry, Wally, Phil.	26	1	222	8.5	30	0

t=Touchdown

KICKOFF RETURNS

YARDS PER RETURN
AFC: 27.6 Horace Ivory, New England (36 returns, 992 yards)
NFC: 25.7 Rich Mauti, New Orleans (31 returns, 798 yards)

YARDS
NFC: 1184 Eddie Payton, Minnesota
AFC: 1070 Bruce Harper, New York

RETURNS
NFC: 53 Eddie Payton, Minnesota
AFC: 49 Bruce Harper, New York

LONGEST
NFC: 101 yards James Owens, San Francisco vs. Detroit, November 2 (TD)
AFC: 98 yards Horace Ivory, New England vs. Baltimore, October 19 (TD)

TOUCHDOWNS
NFC: Drew Hill, Los Angeles vs. Detroit, September 7 (98 yards); Keith Nord, Minnesota vs. Washington, November 2 (70 yards); James Owens, San Francisco vs. Detroit, November 2 (101 yards); Dave Williams, Chicago vs. Detroit, November 27 (95 yards); Ray Williams, Detroit vs. Tampa Bay, December 14 (91 yards)
AFC: Horace Ivory, New England vs. Baltimore, October 19 (98 yards); Derrick Jensen, Oakland vs. New York Giants, December 21 (33 yards); Arthur Whittington, Oakland vs. Cincinnati, November 9 (90 yards)

TEAM CHAMPION
AFC: 22.9 New England (56 returns, 1281 yards)
NFC: 22.4 New Orleans (88 returns, 1973 yards)

TOP TEN KICKOFF RETURNERS

	No	Yards	Avg	Long	TD
Ivory, Horace, N.E.	36	992	27.6	t98	1
Mauti, Rich, N.O.	31	798	25.7	52	0
Williams, Dave, Chi.	27	666	24.7	t95	1
Owens, James, S.F.	31	726	23.4	t101	1
Lewis, Will, Sea.	25	585	23.4	54	0
Green, Roy, St.L.	32	745	23.3	37	0
Brunson, Larry, Den.	40	923	23.1	53	0
Wright, Keith, Clev.	25	576	23.0	50	0
Carson, Carlos, K.C.	40	917	22.9	47	0
Rogers, Jimmy, N.O.	41	930	22.7	88	0

AFC—INDIVIDUALS

	No	Yards	Avg	Long	TD
Ivory, Horace, N.E.	36	992	27.6	t98	1
Lewis, Will, Sea.	25	585	23.4	54	0
Brunson, Larry, Den.	40	923	23.1	53	0
Wright, Keith, Clev.	25	576	23.0	50	0
Carson, Carlos, K.C.	40	917	22.9	47	0
Glasgow, Nesby, Balt.	33	743	22.5	44	0
Pollard, Frank, Pitt.	22	494	22.5	34	0
Dessillieu, Don, Mia.	40	890	22.3	87	0
Harper, Bruce, N.Y.J.	49	1070	21.8	35	0
Hall, Dino, Clev.	32	691	21.6	40	0

NFC—INDIVIDUALS

	No	Yards	Avg	Long	TD
Mauti, Rich, N.O.	31	798	25.7	52	0
Williams, Dave, Chi.	27	666	24.7	t95	1
Owens, James, S.F.	31	726	23.4	t101	1
Green, Roy, St.L.	32	745	23.3	37	0
Rogers, Jimmy, N.O.	41	930	22.7	88	0
Jones, James, Dall.	32	720	22.5	41	0
Payton, Eddie, Minn.	53	1184	22.3	59	0

Davis, Gary, T.B.	....	44	951	21.6	54	0
Kane, Rick, Det.	....	23	495	21.5	62	0
Suhey, Matt, Chi.	....	19	406	21.4	31	0

t=Touchdown